left hand at the top

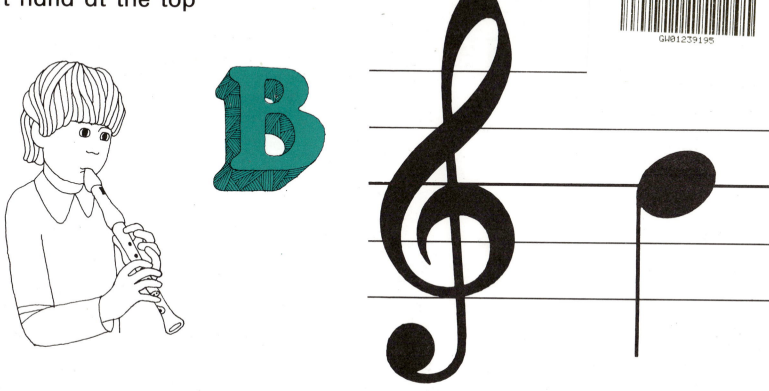

To play B you lift up
most of your fingers,
opening most of the holes.
Press the top finger
of your left hand on to
the top hole.

Close the hole at the
back with your
left thumb.
Play very gently.

Busy bee

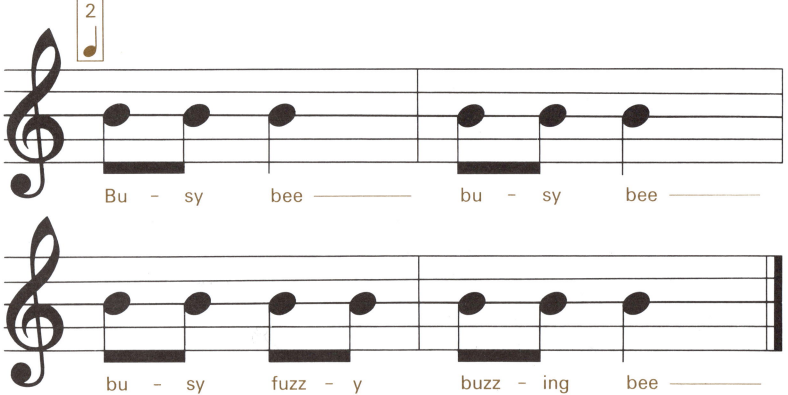

Bu – sy bee ———— bu – sy bee ——

bu – sy fuzz – y buzz – ing bee ——

Make the bed

Make the bed shake the bed

turn the matt – ress o – ver.

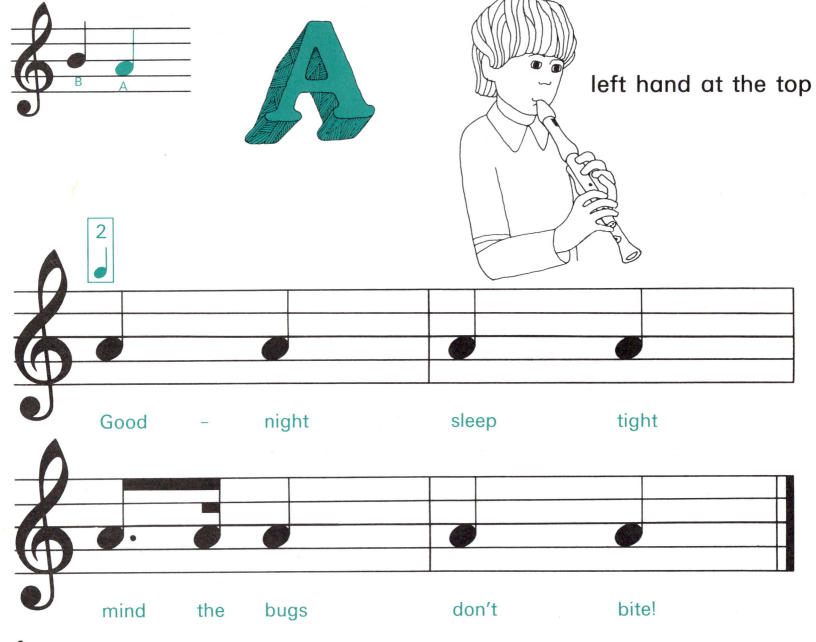

left hand at the top

Good – night   sleep   tight

mind   the   bugs   don't   bite!

4

Big A, little a

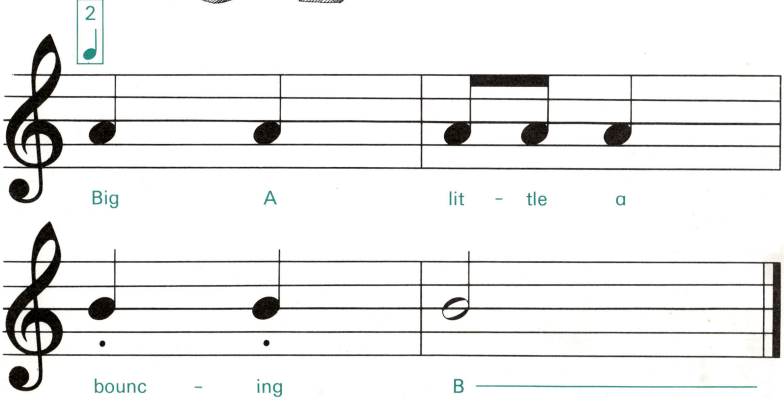

Big   A   lit – tle   a

bounc – ing   B

whisper
the cat's in the cupboard and can't see me.

left hand at the top

One two three ——— Mo-ther caught a flea ———

Put it in the tea-pot made a cup of tea ———

6

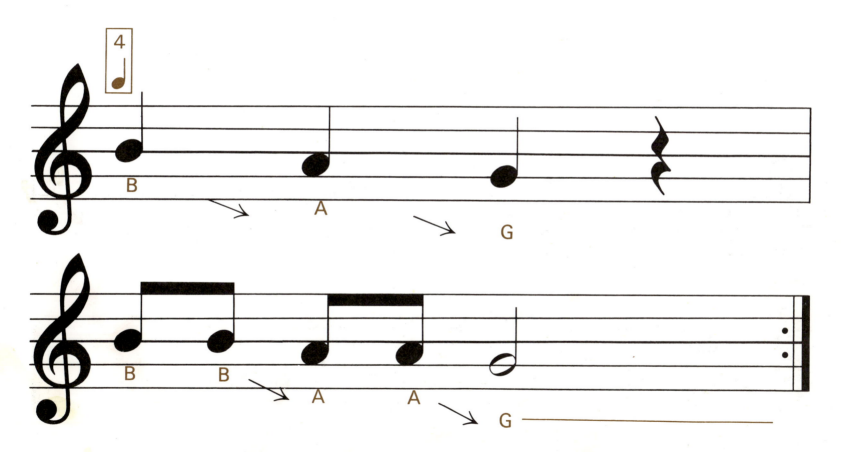

Rain, rain go away

2

Rain   rain   go   a – way.

Come   on   mo – ther's   wash – ing   day.

Boat song

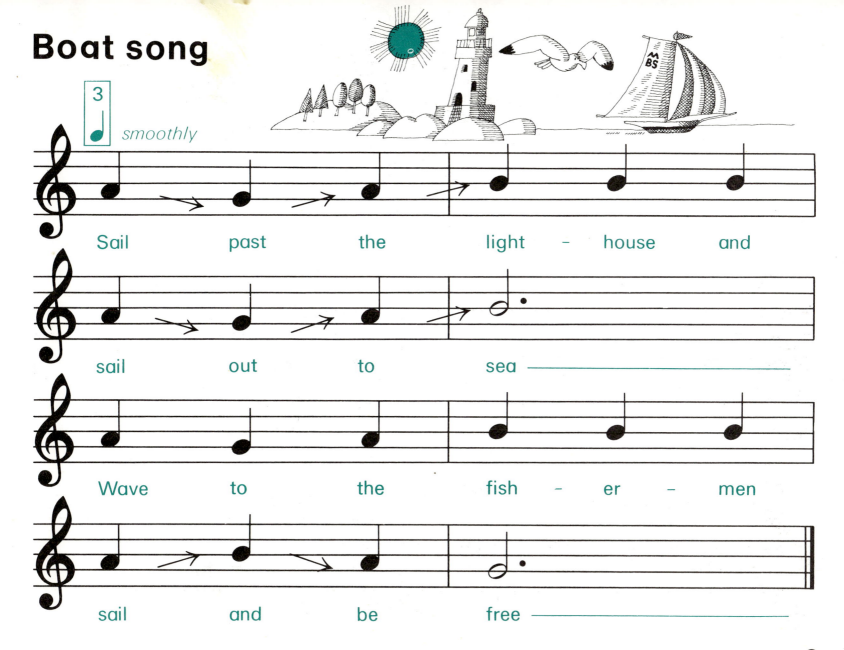

Sail   past   the   light – house   and

sail   out   to   sea ———

Wave   to   the   fish – er – men

sail   and   be   free ———

Tick, tack, toe

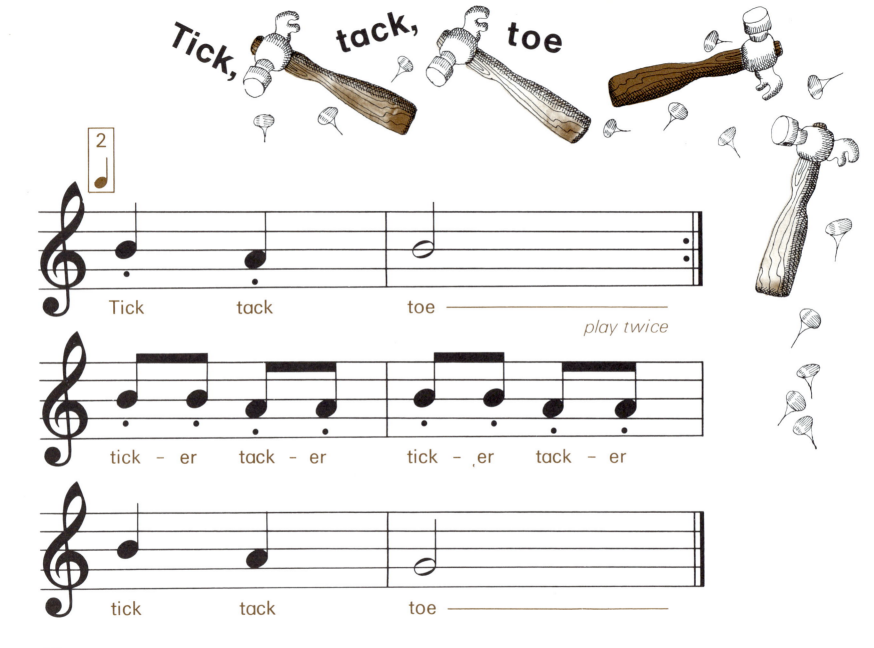

2

Tick   tack   toe

play twice

tick – er   tack – er   tick – er   tack – er

tick   tack   toe

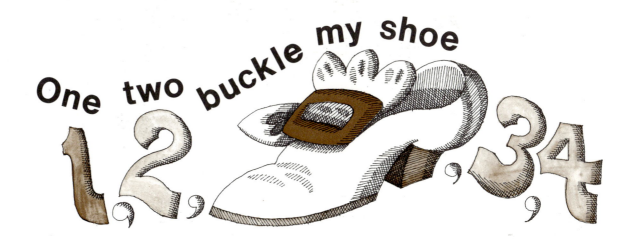

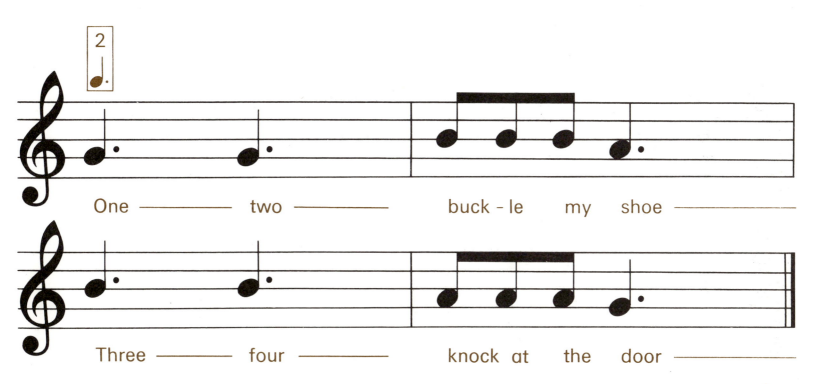

One ———— two ———— buck - le my shoe ————

Three ———— four ———— knock at the door ————

better,

Good,

Best

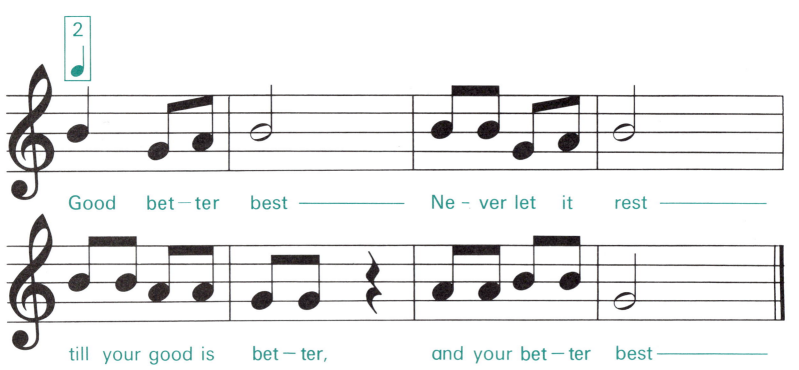

Good bet—ter best ———— Ne - ver let it rest ————

till your good is bet—ter, and your bet—ter best ————

Jack be nimble

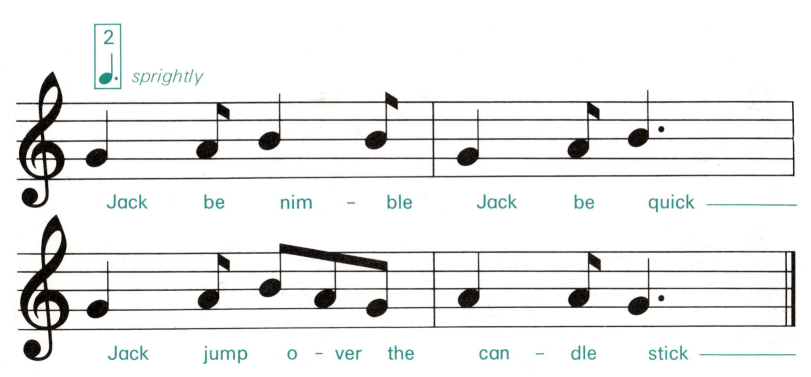

Jack be nim - ble Jack be quick ———

Jack jump o - ver the can - dle stick ———

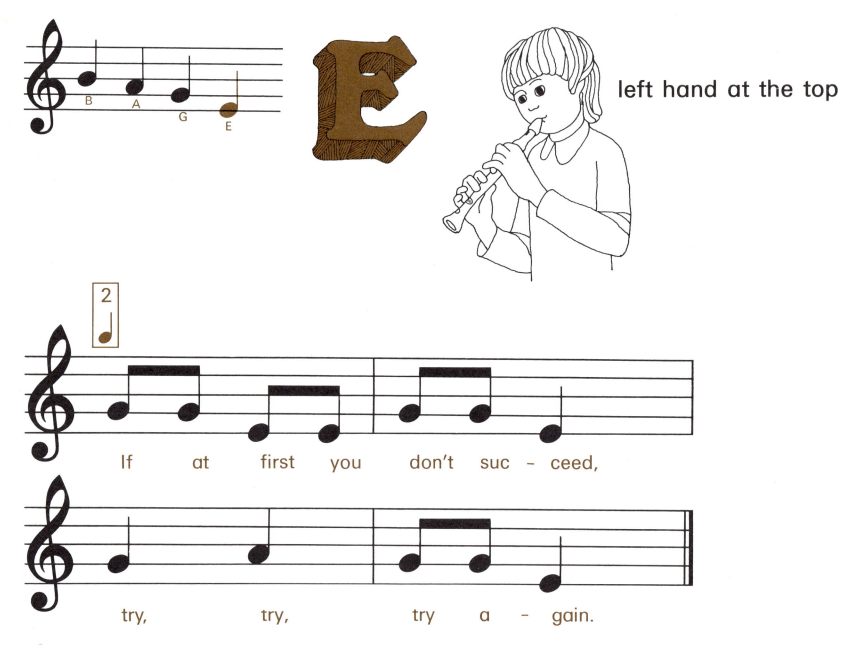

left hand at the top

If at first you don't suc - ceed,

try, try, try a - gain.

14

Swing boats

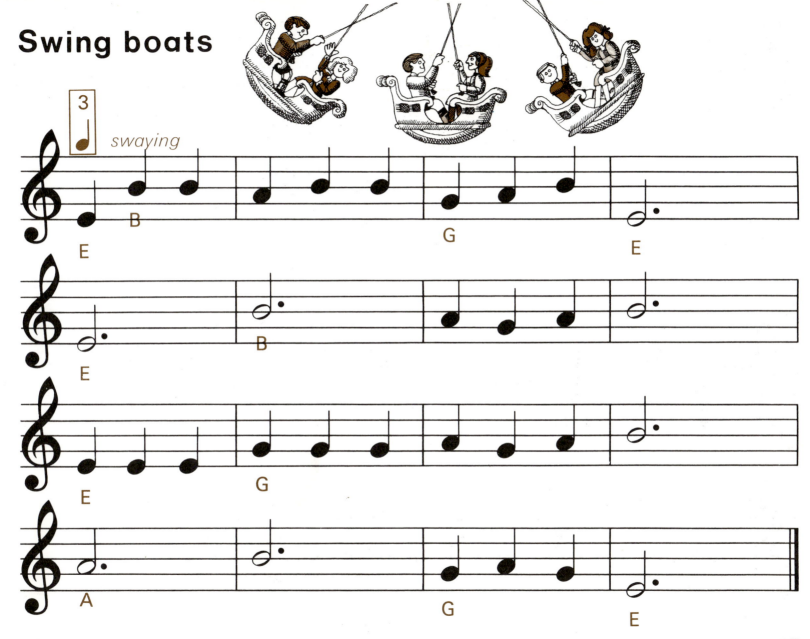

One, two, three, four

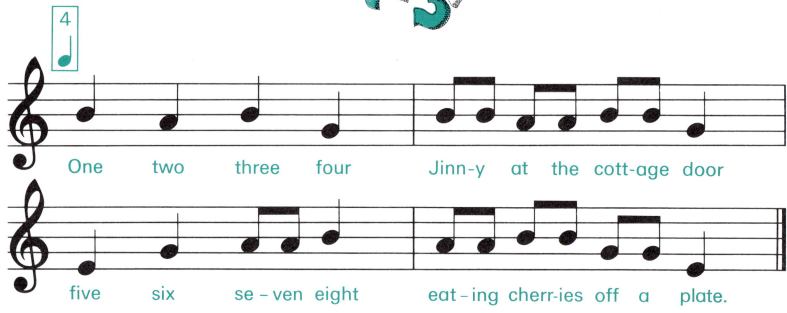

One   two   three   four   Jinn-y   at   the   cott-age   door

five   six   se – ven   eight   eat - ing   cherr-ies   off   a   plate.

By the lake

The snail

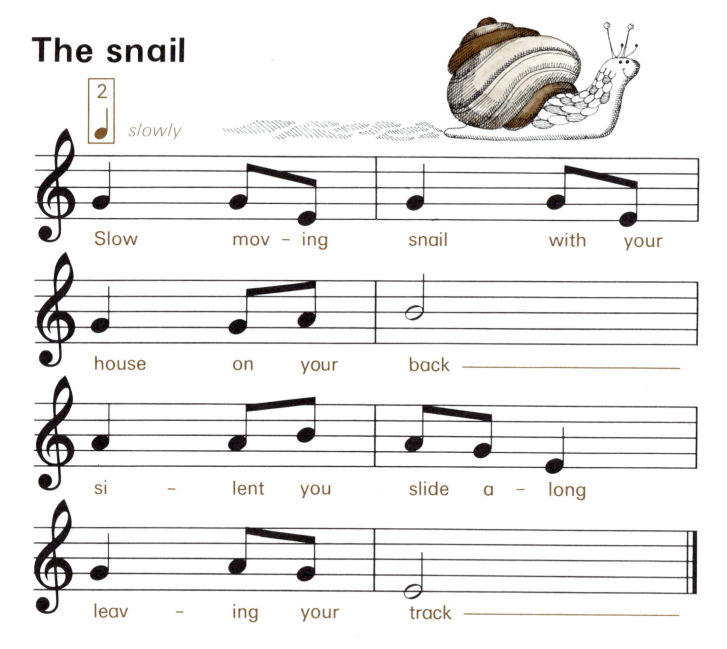

Slow mov - ing snail with your

house on your back ——

si - lent you slide a - long

leav - ing your track ——

18

The frog

Hopp – ing   hopp – ing   lit – tle   frog

jump – ing   from   the   moss – y   log

in – to   wa – ter   green   and   cool

down   in – to   the   deep   pool.

19

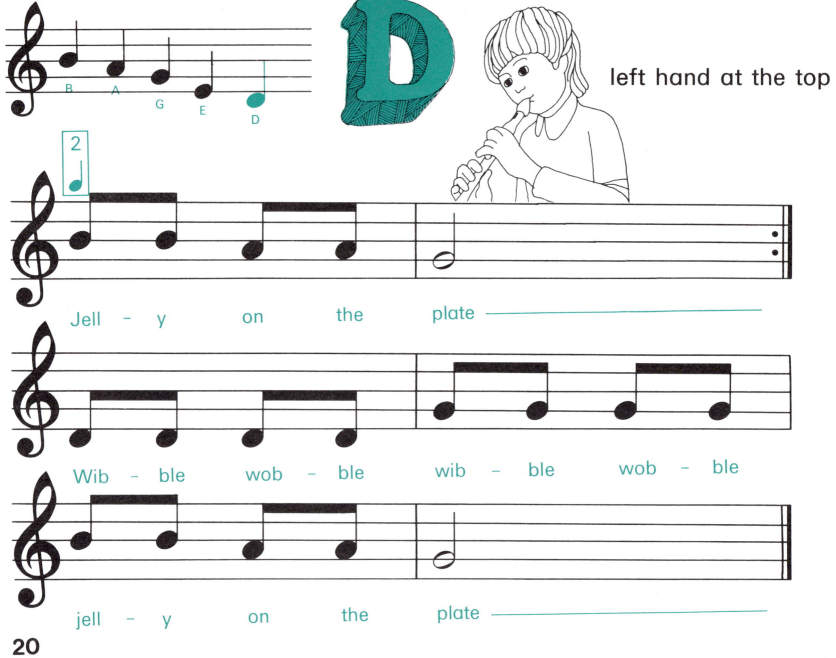

left hand at the top

Jell - y   on   the   plate ———

Wib - ble   wob - ble   wib - ble   wob - ble

jell - y   on   the   plate ———

Sad old clown

Teddy bear

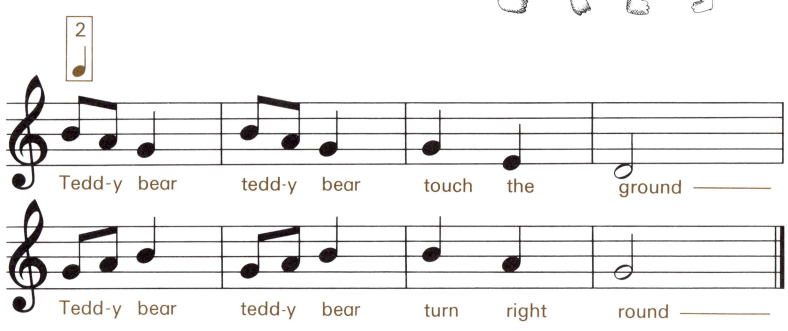

Tedd-y bear   tedd-y bear   touch   the   ground ——

Tedd-y bear   tedd-y bear   turn   right   round ——

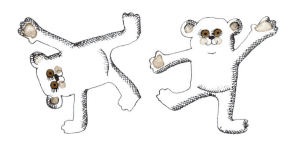

Bugle calls

4

boldly

Come to the cook - house door ———————

Fish and chips for four ———————

One saus-age roll and some soup in a bowl, or a

big juic-y bone on the floor ———————

Two little dicky birds

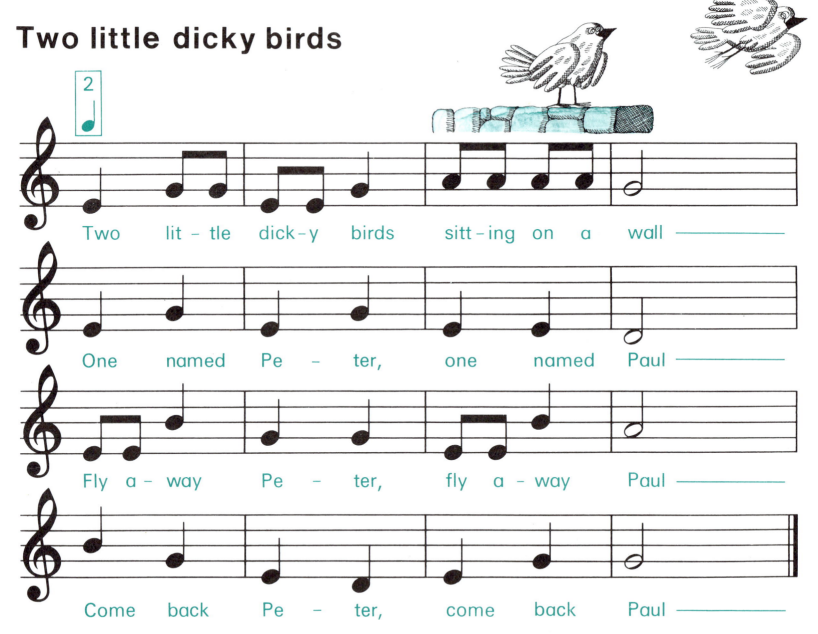

Two lit – tle dick-y birds sitt –ing on a wall —————

One named Pe – ter, one named Paul —————

Fly a – way Pe – ter, fly a – way Paul —————

Come back Pe – ter, come back Paul —————